Written and designed by Lucy Thuo

Illustrations:
- Primary Illustrator for all portraits Olexandra Sirko
- Picture of Queen Victoria by Rocel Hernandez
- Anglo-Saxon by Chenitha Bandara
- Children illustrated by Mus Illustrations and Blue Ring Media

Other Images:
- Photo of HMT Empire Windrush by Royal Navy official photographer, Public domain, via Wikimedia Commons
- Picture of Bill Richmond, Public domain, via Wikimedia Commons
- Pictures of Fanny Eaton, Public domain, via Wikimedia Commons

Copyright © Thuo Books, 2024
All rights reserved.

No part of this book can be reproduced in any form or by written, electronic or mechanical, including photocopying, recording, or by any information retrieval system without written permission in writing by the author.

Published by Thuo Books

Printed by Ingram Spark

Although every precaution has been taken in the preparation of this book, the publisher and author assume no responsibility for errors or omissions. Neither is any liability assumed for damages resulting from the use of information contained herein.

ISBN: 978-1-917762-09-0

CONTENTS PAGE

Introduction	7
Migration	8
A Brief History of Slavery in Britain	9
The British Empire and Colonies	10
The World Wars and Windrush	11
The Ivory Bangle Lady	15
Ellen More	16
John Blanke	17
Catalina de Motril	18
Ignatius Sancho	19
Francis Barber	20
John Ystumllyn	21
Dido Elizabeth Belle	22
Bill Richmond	23
Mary Seacole	24
Peter McLagan	25
Fanny Eaton	26
Sarah Forbes Bonetta	27
Walter Tull	28
George Roberts	29
Robbie Clarke	30
Arthur Roberts	31
Learie Constantine	32
Adelaide Hall	33
Johnny Smythe	34
Princess Ademola	35
Ulric Cross	36
Lilian Bader	37
Billy Strachan	38
Final Thoughts	39

To my husband and children,
who are my heroes and the inspiration for
writing this book.

Introductory Pages

Introduction

Throughout history, Black Britons have shown great initiative and courage, despite often facing great adversity. This book shares the amazing stories of some of these Black Britons in a child-centred, bite-size and visually-appealing approach aimed to encourage children's curiosity about history and inspire the next generation of Black British heroes.

Key terms

It is impossible to write a book about Black British history without covering some key terms first, such as migration and slavery. We cover these terms first as they form a foundation for understanding the rest of the book.

This book is an introduction to the subject of Black British history for children. While subjects in this book can be very emotive, these are addressed with care to try to keep it at a level appropriate for children.

Migration

Throughout history, groups of people have moved from place to place. This movement is called migration. A lot of people living in Britain would find that their family originally came from somewhere other than Britain if you went back far enough. Black Britons would have originally come from Africa. Early Black Britons often travelled to the Caribbean or America before coming to Britain. This migration was most frequently due to the transatlantic slave trade.

A lot of people choose to migrate for better lives. However, sometimes people are forced to migrate to benefit other people.

The Transatlantic Slave Trade

The transatlantic slave trade is an example of this forced movement of people. In fact, it was the largest ever recorded movement of people, with 12.5 million people being moved against their will.

That is the same as taking everyone living in Wales four times over!

It was one of the worst crimes against humanity. Luckily, people were brave and spoke out against slavery and it was stopped in Britain in 1833. A big word for stopped is abolished.

A Brief History of Slavery in Britain

From AD 43 to AD 410, Romans ruled Britain. Slavery happened a lot in this period of history. Around one in five people in the Roman Empire were slaves. They were most often white men expected to do lots of hard work.

After the Romans, slavery continued in the Anglo-Saxon era. The word Briton at that time meant the same thing as slave, as the invading Anglo-Saxons enslaved the people they had conquered.

In 1066, William the Conqueror invaded. This period is called the Norman era. At this time, most slaves became serfs instead and worked the land for the lord of the manor.

In the 14th century, there was a pandemic called the Black Death, which was followed by the Peasants' Revolt because the serfs were unhappy.

In the reign of Tudor Queen Elizabeth I, English ships began to capture slaves from Africa and take them to America.

In the Stuart period, the slave trade grew. It took till 1833 for slavery to be abolished in Britain.

The British Empire and Colonies

There have been many empires throughout history. Empires that became very powerful include the Roman Empire and the much later British Empire. A country gains an empire when it takes control of other countries.

During the reign of Elizabeth I, explorers started going to America and claiming places to be under England's authority.

The first successful colony was during the reign of James I. You may already know this story because the settlers included a man called John Smith and they met a girl called Pocahontas.

Britain kept adding more and more countries to its empire until the 20th century. At this point, the British Empire contained 400 million people and was the biggest empire in history.

The World Wars and Windrush

About 100 years ago there were two wars that meant that a lot of the world was fighting each other.

In the First World War, Britain joined the fight between Austria-Hungary and Serbia. They did this because countries have friends, just like people do. When countries are friends they call it being allies. When Austria-Hungary's ally Germany invaded Belgium, Britain and its allies (including France and Russia) ended up fighting Germany and Austria-Hungary to protect their allies.

While Britain and its allies won the First World War, war against Germany happened again in 1939. This is called the Second World War.

The countries within the British Empire, including countries in Africa and the Caribbean, played a key role in helping Britain's war efforts in these two world wars.

After the Second World War

After the Second World War, Britain was needing rebuilding as it had been bombed. The British government allowed people from the Caribbean to come to live and work in Britain.

The first ship to bring people was called the Empire Windrush. The people arrived in Tilbury in 1948. However, life for these people was challenging. The weather was a lot worse than they were used to and they found that people were not always welcoming, even to war heroes.

Inspirational Black Britons

The Ivory Bangle Lady

The Ivory Bangle Lady was a wealthy lady that lived in Roman Britain during the 4th century AD. The Ivory Bangle Lady was probably originally from North Africa. She had both black and white ancestors, making her mixed race. Both England and North Africa were part of the Roman Empire. It was possible for people to travel around the Empire.

Wealthy Roman woman liked to dress well, with pretty jewellery showing their status. She wore black and white bangles. The black bangles were jet from Yorkshire, and the white were ivory, probably from Africa. Some of her possessions included:

ivory and jet bangles

silver and bronze pendants

blue beads and yellow earrings

a mirror

a glass jug

The Romans left Britain in the 5th century AD. At this point, the connection between North Africa and Britain stopped.

Did you know?
The Ivory Bangle Lady was found in York. During Roman times, York was called Eboracum.

Ellen More

Ellen More was one of two women taken from a Portuguese ship as slaves and gifted to the Scottish King James IV by the Bartons, a famous Scottish seafaring family.

The women were treated well and given beautiful clothes. They were part of the royal household of Henry VIII's sister Margaret, who was married to James IV.

Ellen was the 'Black Lady' in two tournaments held at Edinburgh Castle in 1507 and 1508 called 'The jousting of the wild knight for the black lady'. The King secretly dressed as the 'Wild Knight' and acted as her champion as he fought.

Did you know?
James IV's great-grandson was James VI, the first King of Scotland to also be King of England (as James I).

John Blanke

John Blanke was a trumpeter for two famous kings of England: Henry VII, the first Tudor King of England, and his son Henry VIII.

John featured twice in the Westminster Tournament Roll, which was a really long picture showing a joust that Henry VIII organised. A joust is where two people fight on horseback, each with a long pointed weapon called a lance. The roll measured about 60 foot, which is the same length as a bowling alley!

Did you know?
The trumpeters that played during the Westminster Tournament got ten times their regular wage that day.

Catalina de Motril

Catalina was originally from Motril, Granada. She came with Catherine of Aragon from Spain when Catherine came to England to marry Arthur Tudor. After Arthur died, Catherine married Henry VIII.

Did you know?
Catalina is the Spanish version of Catherine. She would not have been born with the name Catalina but she would have been called that when she started working for Catherine of Aragon. This was the traditional way of naming enslaved people in Spain at that time in history.

There were no slaves in England during Tudor times, so Catalina would not have been a slave when she came to England.

Tudor royalty did not make their own beds. Catalina's job was to make the royal beds for them.

Ignatius Sancho

Ignatius was born on a slave ship. He was taken to be a slave in New Granada. When he was two, he was taken to Greenwich, where he worked for three sisters. He did not like this life and, when he was 18, he decided to run away.

He was a talented writer and wrote against the slave trade. He became known as a writer of letters, as well as writing plays and musical compositions.

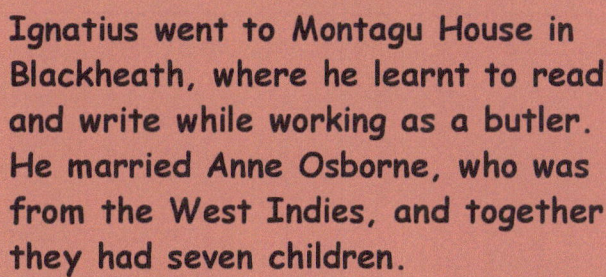

Ignatius went to Montagu House in Blackheath, where he learnt to read and write while working as a butler. He married Anne Osborne, who was from the West Indies, and together they had seven children.

With the help of Montagu, Ignatius set up a grocery shop, where he made many friends who came to buy from his shop. Because he owned a shop and his own home, he was allowed to vote. He was the first man of Black heritage known to have voted in a British parliamentary election.

Francis Barber

Francis Barber was born around 1742. He started life in Jamaica as a slave. When he was about seven years old, his owner Colonel Bathurst took him to London and he then attended school in Yorkshire until he was 10. He went to work for Dr Johnson as a helper, as his wife had died.

When Colonel Bathurst died, Francis was given his freedom in his will. He spent some time in the Navy before returning to Dr Johnson, who paid for him to continue his education.

Dr Johnson opposed slavery, unlike many at the time.

When Francis married and had a son, he named him Samuel, the same first name as Dr Johnson, in his honour.

Did you know?
The dictionary written by Dr Johnson took eight years to write and it contained 42,773 words.

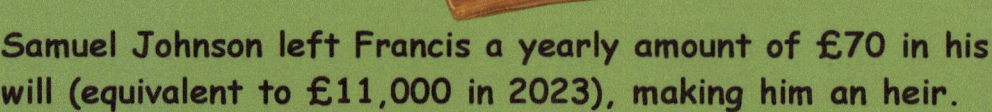

Samuel Johnson left Francis a yearly amount of £70 in his will (equivalent to £11,000 in 2023), making him an heir.

John Ystumllyn

John was born in 1738, although his parents and where he was from are a mystery. What is known is that he ended up at the Ystumllyn estate in a place called Criccieth in Wales with the Wynn family, who christened him John Ystumllyn.

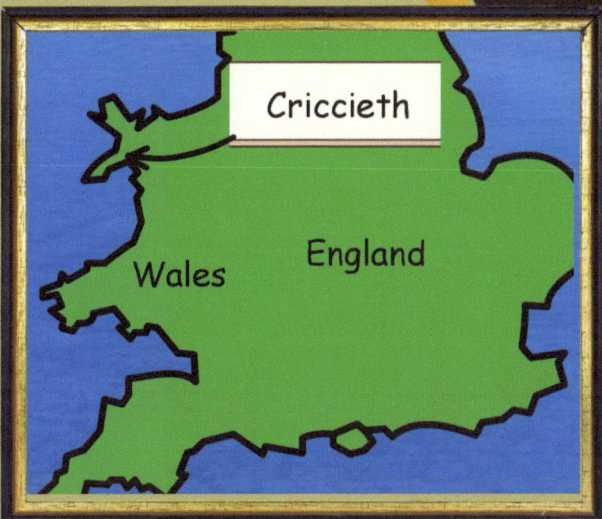

John became a talented gardener, who was well-liked by the locals. He even fell in love with a maid called Margaret and ran away to get married to her in 1768. They had seven children together.

When John returned to the Wynn family, he was gifted a cottage and garden.

Did you know?
In 2021, John Ystumllyn was the first person of ethnic minority heritage to have a variety of rose named after them in the UK.

Dido Elizabeth Belle

Dido Elizabeth Belle was born in 1761 to Sir John Lindsay, a naval officer, and Maria Belle, an enslaved woman in the West Indies.

Although Dido was born into slavery, her father wanted a better fate for her. He took her back to England where his uncle William Murray, 1st Earl of Mansfield, and his wife were happy to look after her. They were already looking after their other little great-niece, Lady Elizabeth Murray, who was in their care because her mother had died.

Her great uncle's affection for Dido and his view that slavery was bad significantly influenced some English and Welsh justice rulings at a time when slavery was rampant. Her great uncle's position as Lord Chief Justice of England and Wales helped to bring some justice against slavery. He ruled that slavers could not use force to take enslaved people in England out of the country, through the case of James Somerset. He also played an important role in the case of the Zong slave ship.

Her great uncle left Dido a large sum of money and a yearly payment in his will, making her an heiress.

In 1793, Dido married John Davinier and they had three sons.

Bill Richmond

Bill was born into slavery in New York in 1763. There he caught the attention of Lord Percy, a commander of the British forces, who noticed he was a talented fighter.

In 1777, Lord Percy freed Bill and took him back to Northern England, where he paid for his education. Bill then got an apprenticeship as a cabinet maker in Yorkshire.

In Yorkshire, he married a woman called Mary and they moved to London. In 1795, he was employed by Thomas Pitt for a time before taking up boxing.

Did you know?
Bill became really famous and successful. He was even part of the coronation celebrations for King George IV, Queen Victoria's uncle.

He won 17 of 19 fights and bought a pub with his winning money. He also ran a boxing school which trained people to fight, including the poet Lord Byron.

Mary Seacole

Mary was born in 1805 in Jamaica to a Jamaican mother, who ran a lodging house, and a Scottish father, who was a British soldier. It was from her mother that she became interested in helping to make ill people feel better, as she watched her mother heal people using traditional Jamaican medicine. Mary then practised what she had seen on her doll.

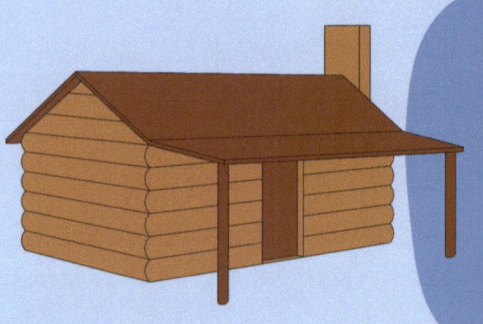

When the Crimean War happened, Mary Seacole was determined to go and nurse wounded soldiers. She went to England to join Florence Nightingale's team but was turned away.

Mary would not let this stop her, so she went on a boat to Crimea. She set up the British Hotel to help wounded soldiers close to the battlefield. Mary even went into the battlefield to help injured soldiers. A journalist visited the British Hotel and wrote about Mary Seacole's wonderful work.

At the end of the war, Mary Seacole was penniless. She had spent all her money saving people's lives. She was visited in England by the same journalist. He wrote an article about Mary's work to raise money for her. They even organised a festival in her honour and Queen Victoria wrote a message praising her for her fantastic work.

Peter McLagan

Peter was born on New Year's Day in 1823 in Guyana, South America. His father (also called Peter McLagan) was a successful sugar plantation owner.

Peter was five when he moved to Scotland with his father and brother. Both Peter and his brother were well-educated and attended Edinburgh University.

In 1865, Peter became the first Black MP in Scotland, in a place called Linlithgowshire. He was re-elected six times, making him the longest-serving Scottish MP during the Victorian era.

At the time Peter was an MP, only men were allowed to vote. Peter supported women gaining the right to vote.

Did you know?
MP stands for Member of Parliament. A Member of Parliament is someone elected by the people of a particular area to represent them in the House of Commons.

Fanny Eaton

Fanny Eaton was born in Jamaica in 1835, just after slavery ended there. Fanny moved to England with her mother as a child. She came to England quite soon after Queen Victoria became queen, meaning that she lived in Victorian England.

Fanny worked as an artist's model and was often one of the main characters in the paintings.
Can you spot her in these paintings?

Did you know?
There were no cars in Victorian England. People travelled by horse-drawn carriages. Fanny married James Eaton, who drove these like a taxi.

Sarah Forbes Bonetta

Sarah Forbes Bonetta was born into a high-ranking family in Yoruba in West Africa. However, she was orphaned and was later captured by the King of Dahomey. When Captain Forbes went to see the King of Dahomey, he saw the young girl, who would have only been about seven at the time. He managed to negotiate her freedom and took her to England.

Did you know?
She was named after the boat she sailed to England on, the HMS Bonetta.

Queen Victoria became Sarah's godmother and took a keen interest in her education and well-being.

When Sarah got married to Captain James Davies, Queen Victoria made sure she had an incredible wedding. They went to Africa and had three children, the first named Victoria in honour of the queen. She also became Queen Victoria's godchild.

Walter Tull

Walter Tull was really talented at football. He became a professional footballer for three English football teams: Clapton, Tottenham Hotspur and Northampton Town. He was also the first person of Black heritage to be signed by Rangers Football Club in Scotland.

When the First World War started, Walter joined the Football Battalion. In 1917, he was made an officer and became one of the first people of Black heritage to lead British troops into battle.

Did you know?
Poppies are used to remember all the brave soldiers that die in wars.

George Roberts

George was born in 1891 in Trinidad and Tobago. When he was a boy, he played with his friends throwing coconuts at each other.

When the First World War started, George became part of the Trinidad Army and moved to England to join the Middlesex Regiment. He used the skills he had learnt as a child to throw back German bombs.

When the Second World War happened, George was too old to fight on the front line but it didn't stop him from being brave. He saved many people's lives as a firefighter during the Blitz. He was awarded a British Empire Medal.

Not only was George a great fighter but he was a great speaker too. He returned to Trinidad and Tobago and encouraged 250 men to become soldiers.

Did you know?
In the first 22 nights of bombing, the firefighters had to put out almost 10,000 fires.

Robbie Clarke

Robbie Clarke was born in 1895 in Jamaica. He came to the UK to help with the First World War. His first job was as an air mechanic.

Did you know?
15,600 Black Caribbean volunteers helped fight in World War 1.

Robbie was then sent to be a driver for an observation balloon company in France. Observation balloons were really important during World War 1 as they allowed for a much better ability to see what the enemy was doing from a height than looking from the ground.

Robbie's dream was to become a pilot. He went back to England to train and became the first pilot of Black heritage to fly for Britain.

There were no mobile phones or internet to communicate during World War 1. The main way to contact your family was by sending letters. Each week, 12 million letters were delivered to soldiers. Robbie wrote to his mother during the war.

Arthur Roberts

Arthur was born in Bristol in 1897 to a father from the West Indies and an English mother. They moved to Scotland, where Arthur did well at school.

Arthur was excited to join the army to fight in the First World War. However, his diary shows that life on the battlefield was harder than he thought it would be.

When Arthur came back from the war, he became a successful engineer and electrician. He got married and lived in Glasgow.

Did you know?
For years, Arthur's diaries were in an attic. They were discovered in 2004, 86 years after the end of the war.

Learie Constantine

Learie was born in Trinidad in 1901. He was part of the West Indies Cricket team before deciding to become a professional cricketer in England.

During the Second World War, Learie worked as a Welfare Officer for factory workers from the West Indies.

Learie also successfully sued a London hotel after they refused to let him and his family stay at the hotel. The case was an important milestone towards racial equality in Britain.

Learie went on to become a lawyer and politician and was Trinidad and Tobago's High Commissioner for the United Kingdom. He was knighted in 1962 and became Sir Learie Constantine. In 1969, he became the United Kingdom's first Black peer when he was made a baron.

Adelaide Hall

Adelaide Hall was an American singer who was very successful in both America and Europe. She married a British sailor and later moved to England. She decided that, rather than go back to America during the Second World War, she would entertain people in England during the Blitz. She later went to Germany to entertain the British troops on the front line.

The word Blitz comes from the German word Blitzkrieg, which means 'lightning war'. The Germans bombed England, especially in industrial areas like London.

Adelaide continued to perform until the 1990s. She entered the Guinness World Records in 2003 for the most enduring recording artist (1927 to 1991). She performed over eight decades.

Did you know?
One evening when London was being bombed, Adelaide was performing at the old Lewisham Hippodrome. She performed for four hours, singing 54 songs before it was safe for people to leave at 3.45 am!

Johnny Smythe

Johnny was one of only six men chosen from Sierra Leone to be trained as an RAF pilot in World War 2. He was great at maths, so he was then trained as a navigator and was soon promoted to being an officer.

He was successful, and completed 26 flights (most only did 12) before being shot down and taken to a prisoner-of-war camp. He was also lucky to escape as one morning the prisoners found that all the German guards had run away during the night, having heard that the Russian Army were coming.

Did you know?
In 1948 he was a senior officer on the Empire Windrush, taking military men back to their home in the Caribbean. However, on arrival, they realized the economy was struggling and the men would have a difficult life there. Johnny organised for them to live in the UK instead.

Princess Ademola

Princess Ademola was born in 1916. She was the daughter of the Alake of Abeokuta, a king in south-west Nigeria.

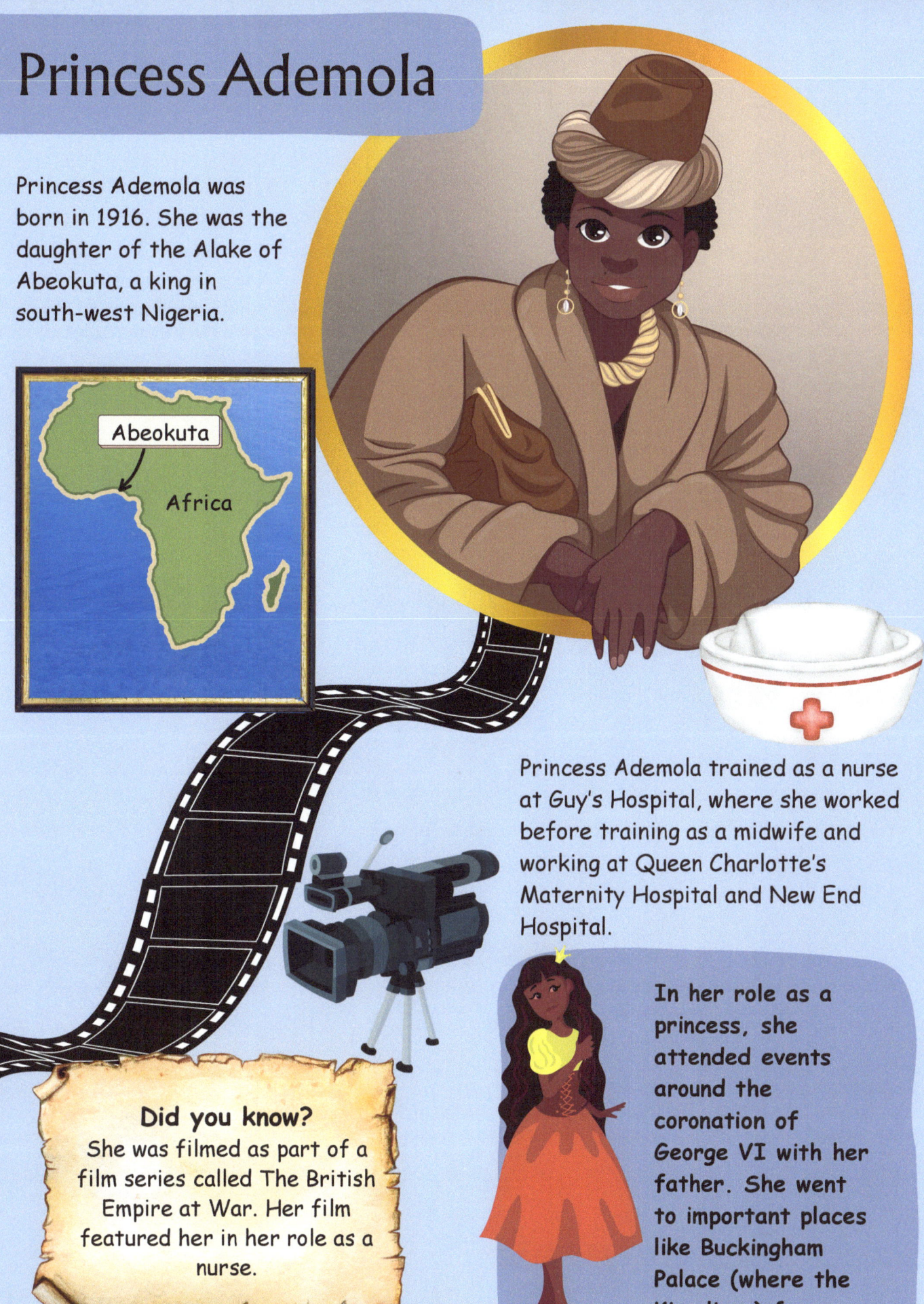

Princess Ademola trained as a nurse at Guy's Hospital, where she worked before training as a midwife and working at Queen Charlotte's Maternity Hospital and New End Hospital.

Did you know?
She was filmed as part of a film series called The British Empire at War. Her film featured her in her role as a nurse.

In her role as a princess, she attended events around the coronation of George VI with her father. She went to important places like Buckingham Palace (where the King lives) for parties.

Ulric Cross

Ulric Cross was born in 1917 in Trinidad. He was a very bright child and scored the best result for a scholarship for free education at St Mary's College. As a teenager, he dreamed of becoming a Flight Lieutenant with the RAF and being awarded a Distinguished Flying Cross.

He decided to travel to England to help with the Second World War. He joined RAF Bomber Command as a navigator and rose to the rank of Squadron Leader. He achieved his dream and was awarded a Distinguished Flying Cross and Distinguished Service Order.

Did you know?

He was part of a very special force of bombers called the Pathfinder Force who flew much lower than normal bombers, flying at 50 feet rather than 25,000 feet. This meant they had only 11 seconds to escape the bombs they had just dropped and get to safety.

As a navigator, he did 80 missions and saved 200 RAF bombers from being shot down.

After the war, he was honoured further for his outstanding work as a judge and diplomat.

Lilian Bader

Lilian was born to a Barbadian father and an Irish mother. Her father was a Merchant Seaman during the First World War. She and her two brothers were orphaned when she was nine years old. She was separated from her brothers and sent to a convent (a place where dedicated Christian women called nuns live) until she was 20.

Lilian was excited to get her first job in an armed forces canteen during the Second World War. However, after seven weeks she sadly lost her job, due to her father being born outside the United Kingdom.

Lilian was still keen to help with the war effort and learned on the radio that the Royal Air Force were taking people of West Indian descent. She trained as an instrument repairer. She went on to become a First Class Airwoman, Leading Aircraftwoman and Corporal.

After the war, Lilian studied and achieved a degree, allowing her to become a teacher.

Billy Strachan

Billy was born in Jamaica in 1921. When the Second World War started, he decided to sell his saxophone and bicycle to pay for his ticket to England.

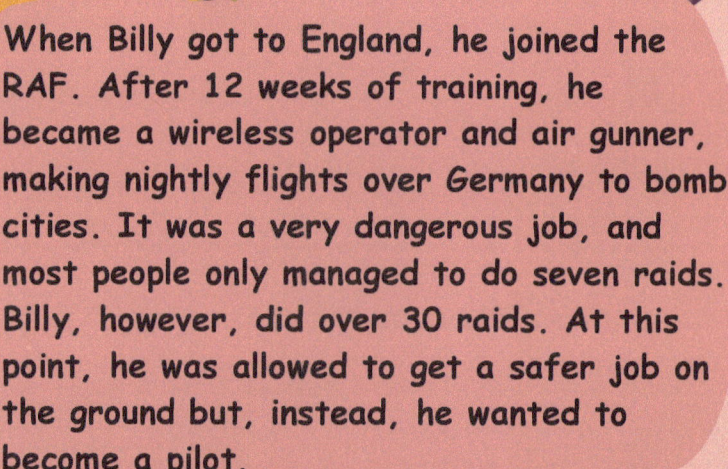

When Billy got to England, he joined the RAF. After 12 weeks of training, he became a wireless operator and air gunner, making nightly flights over Germany to bomb cities. It was a very dangerous job, and most people only managed to do seven raids. Billy, however, did over 30 raids. At this point, he was allowed to get a safer job on the ground but, instead, he wanted to become a pilot.

However, the training to become a pilot was not easy. Billy got injured during training trying to do tricks in the plane. While he was recovering, he married a woman called Joyce Smith. On their honeymoon in Torquay, the Germans bombed their hotel and they were lucky to survive.

When Billy became a pilot, he did 15 more missions and got two promotions to Flying Officer and Flight Lieutenant. However, a near collision with Lincoln Cathedral made him change jobs and he became a racial advisor to the RAF.

After the war, Billy helped set up the London branch of the Caribbean Labour Congress. This set up a committee to help the people who came on the HMS Windrush as they faced challenges of accommodation and employment in the UK.

FINAL THOUGHTS

As we now come to the end of this book, hopefully you have enjoyed reading some of the inspirational stories of Black British heroes. It is worth spending a minute to reflect. Whether or not you are Black British, there are strong themes found in the lives of these heroes that you can take with you, such as bravery, perseverance, pursuing your dreams and not letting anything stand in the way of the great things that every one of us is capable of.

As you read the book, you may resonate with people who have similar talents to you, be it music, writing, sport, or qualities you have as a person, like being caring or determined. These talents are not defined by how we look but who we are as a person inside. Everyone is special and talented in their own unique way. We hope this book helps you on your path to discovering your own special talents.

Britain is a country that is multicultural. As you can see from this book, this extends far back in time before your great great great grandparents were born, so far back that most people can't even trace their family history that far back. This is something to be celebrated. As a country, we are made up of a wonderful group of people with different life stories, experiences, traditions and appearances.

www.ingramcontent.com/pod-product-compliance
Lightning Source LLC
Chambersburg PA
CBHW041118070526
44584CB00002B/203